THE WILD BRANCH

A Book of Poetry, Art, Haiku, and Lyrics

by Lynn Sorlie

"The abundant rains
Have brought out many creatures
Like that little fox."

THE WILD BRANCH

by Lynn Sorlie

Poetry Written for Small Press Magazines and State Poetry Organizations

"Never destroy any aspect of personality, for what you think is the wild branch may be the heart of the tree."
Mrs. Henry George

Adventures in Poetry (TX), Amber (N.S.), Bardic Echoes (MI) Constructive Action Newsletter (NY), Cotyledon (AL), Dragonfly Haiku Quarterly (OR), Driftwood East (RI), Encore (NM), Fine Arts Press (TN), Happy Publishers (CO), Harbor Lights (MN), Hoosier Challenger-Gusto (OH), Japan Forum (Japan), Jean's Journal, Masters of Modern Poetry (Italy), Modern Images (IL), POET International (India), Quintessence (LA), and Special Song. Since 2000, I've been published in the Minnesota Moccasin, League of Minnesota Poets magazine. I belong to that state organization and Bella Vista Writer's Guild, in Arkansas.

Copyright by Lynn Sorlie 2013

Credits for Doodles and Drawings by Lynn Sorlie

Mother and Baby at a Picnic, photo; "Dining and Dancing at the Two Notes"; The Hairdresser doodle; Whimsical Dots; Sandcastles drawing; London Bridge, transported and restored, Lake Havasu, AZ, photo; 4th of July at Park Point Before the Fireworks, photo; Bee and Flower doodle; Rainbow; Corn Husk Doll; Snowshoe Bunnies, illustration.

Hairdresser

I think it was my Aunt Helen who said,
"Keep on with your writing."
It's like Mrs. O'Leary said,
"Marriage is for keeps, you know."
I have tried very hard to do both.
Hanging onto John was like hanging
Onto a tiger's tail. He never made
It easy, but then, neither did I.

CONTENTS

	Page
Title Page	1
Copyright Page	2
Credits for doodles and drawings	3
Acknowledgement Page	4
Contents	5
Part I, Poetry, Photo	7
The Archaeologist, Time	8
A Good Friend, Lyric	9
Big City	10
Circles	11
Drawing, "Dining and Dancing at The Two Notes"	12
Fountains, and In So Many Ways	13
Fred the Bird, and What We Can Do	14
Hildegard	15
Inequities	16
The Laundromat	17
Lilacs in May	18
Lo and Behold, and Death of a Relationship	19
Marriage	20
The Maze, and Twitch, Twitch, Twitch	22
Moments	23
The Hairdresser Doodle	24
Morning Glory	25
The New Snowfall	26
Nurture	27
Obstacles	28
On Second Thought	29
Opportunity When It Knocks, and Courage	30
The Other Side of Sun-Night, and The Island	31
Peace Is Elusive, and True Gifts	33
Pebbles, and Whimsical Dots	34
Photographs for an Album, and Paradox	35
The Primrose	36

Red, and Valentine	37
Reflections, Lyric	38
Renewal	39
Rikki's Chinchilla Factory	40
Sandcastles Drawing	41
Sandcastles, in English	42
Sandcastles, in French	43
Some Guests	44
Spring Fever	45
The Threshold	46
Weather Shift, and Snow Weave	47
The Well, and Called Back to Reality	48
Part II, Essay, Photo	50
Short Essay, The Meaning of Poetry	51
More to be Said About Poetry	53
Part III, Haiku, Photo	54
Acknowledgment	55
Bee and Flower Doodle	56
Spring Haiku	57
Rainbow drawing	64
Summer Haiku	65
Cornhusk Doll drawing	80
Fall Haiku	81
Snowshoe Bunnies drawing	88
Winter Haiku	89

Cover: Loring Park Photo, Lynn Sorlie

PART I, POETRY

Arranged Alphabetically
With Minor Exceptions

THE ARCHAEOLOGIST

He digs down through each strata
Of earth's encapsuled time.
Nothing too small eludes him;
With a fine brush he works;
And during his digs he finds
Answers and enigmas
In nature's storehouse
Of time and patience.
Backward he goes through time,
Downward he goes through dirt,
Through living rooms, burial sites,
Palaces and streets,
Downward until…
History becomes prehistory,
Until…all trace of life is gone,
And the whispering winds prevail.

The Moccasin, 2000

TIME

Our strongest ally, liberator, friend,
Our strongest enemy, jailor, foe,
That seems so endlessly stretched out,
Yet sometimes presses so….

The Moccasin, 2010

A GOOD FRIEND

You're in a rut
Get out, you got in
With your door always shut,
With a frown, not a grin.
It's a terrible waste
To rarely come out;
Change your toothpaste,
Maybe laugh, maybe shout!
Live with more life
Than you have in the past,
With more challenge, more strife,
Or a love meant to last.
They may find you one day,
And bury you under;
Since they found you this way,
It is you made the blunder.
How can you be sure
That they'll know you're alive!
You're so rich, yet so poor…
I'll be back here by five.

The Moccasin, 2007, Lyric

BIG CITY

Kaleidoscope images whirling
Lights streaking
Horns honking
Sirens wailing
Whistles blowing
Buying and selling
Window shoppers leisurely admiring
Much too much money
Frantic pedestrians in pursuit of it
Passing them by
Cabs dropping off passengers
Picking up new ones, going out into
The mainstream of the city
Black leather evening, wet pavement
Kinky lights and colors, mirrored
Hurrying to and from
Shows and sideshows
Such a hurry-scurry
For the stuff that dreams are made of.

Encore, 1976, The Varieties, Act X, Scene 2
The Moccasin, 2005

CIRCLES

Circles spiraling around,
Making up our Milky Way,
Sound that also spirals from
Tapes and CD's that we play,
Skaters twirling on the ice
Make more circles as they spin,
Pilots circling a field
Patiently wait to come in.
Current eddies in a stream,
Weather fronts that circle 'round,
Circles in a piece of pipe,
Yo-yos, tops, thread tightly wound,
Bracelets, gameballs, powderpuffs,
Circus rings, tires, ferris wheels,
Porch lights with gnats flying 'round,
Buttons, bottle caps, film reels,
Circles in a braided rug,
Circles in a mutual hug!

International Library of Poetry, 2003
The Moccasin, 2008

"Dining and Dancing at the Two Notes" — Lynn Sorlie

FOUNTAINS

I've seen the dried leaves
Gathering on the bottom of fountains.

This one has been abandoned,
No longer kept up
At the owner's expense,
No one to come and sit by it
And hear the water's cool splash
like a laugh.

So something is missing --
not just the water, or the laugh,
but those who would come.

The Moccasin, 2003

IN SO MANY WAYS

You fill my days, my dreams, my heart in so many ways...
The hours we share are precious hours beyond compare,
Each time I learn to know you more, the more I yearn...
You know that I will love you more as the years go by.

Lyrical Treasures, Classic and Modern
Fine Arts Press, Kingsport, Tennessee

FRED THE BIRD

Ruffled flutter, but no chatter,
Sad, forlorn was he.
Cat's a killer, nothing chiller,
Bird fell from a tree.
Heard a cheeping, cat not sleeping,
Light on in the yard.
Tiny sparrow, escape narrow,
Life has been too hard.
Brought our small pet to a tall vet,
Known these parts around.
Fred looks better in his sweater,
And his wing is bound.

The Moccasin, 2004

WHAT WE CAN DO

Even in hard times
We can do little acts of kindness,
That chase away the shadows
Of circumstance.
When hard times come,
We can do fulfilling things
To fill a need.
We build that way,
Brick upon mortar,
Mortar upon brick.

HILDEGARD

Meet Hildegard, our St. Bernard,
Romping around the yard
(a small, fluffy pup, you know
a year ago).

What is she doing, excavating?
If it were our flowerless garden,
We wouldn't care.
We don't dare plant flowers
With Hildegard there
(but not our new sod!)

One day in mood of rose,
She jumped playfully at a man,
In friendship, nipped his nose!
Six stitches it took; in short,
We'll have it out in court.
Bruised by her warm caress,
The man was quite a mess!

Anyone want Hildegard?
Hil-HILDEGARD!
With the whole line of laundry in tow,
Romping around the yard!

INEQUITIES

There is never enough
MONEY,
There is never enough
LOVE,
There is never enough
TIME,
There is never enough
FOOD,
There is always some shortage
Somewhere on the earth,
And this varies from time
To time, place to place
And people to people.
Love answers all of these needs.
With love, I mean if everybody loved,
There would be ENOUGH
(money, food, time),
enough for all.

The Moccasin, 2006

THE LAUNDROMAT

Without the sensibility
To understand what is happening,
Clothes are tossed, revolving,
Reversed, agitated, spinned,
Rinsed and dried.

I stare at the colors until
My mind is numb.
I wonder how many of us feel
A little bit like that,
As if life is giving us
A pounding.

I suppose what counts
Is that we learn something
From all this.
We need to get through whatever
Event, issue, problem troubles us.
"One rinse, or two?"
One is enough for most of us.

LILACS IN MAY

Purple honeysuckle shaped flowers
Clustered on a stem
In plentiful display…
Lilac blooms arching over fences
Cups, glass jars, tin cans
For mother.
Purple cones of fragrance
Cool green leaves…
Lush and plentiful
Exotic in hue
Gracious and welcome in any home
Something for mother.
The gentle thieves
With only love to blame
Break off each tender branch
And rush home with their treasure,
"Mother, these are for you."

Encore, 1978, The Varieties, Act XI, Scene 2
The Moccasin, 2001

LO AND BEHOLD

God bless you, for I have seen
The rebirth of old hopes,
Like green grass growing
From a burned forest floor.
The death of a forest is a tragedy
Likened to the death of dreams.
In somebody's heart today,
A bright green shoot is springing up.
I thought it was impossible,
But miracles still happen
In burned-out lives.

The Moccasin, 2006

DEATH OF A RELATIONSHIP

I am now terminal
In your life and consciousness.
Pardon me if, every now and then,
There is a little beep beep beep
In mine.

The Moccasin, 2000

MARRIAGE

The Raft

We are a raft,
Not sturdy in itself
But bound together
By strong rope, barnacles,
And seaweed; still,
There is a point
Where something gives way,
And it is now. Sorry!

Old Glue

We are two pieces
Of dissimilar material
Bonded together
With the strongest glue;
But even so, we must
Admit to failure
In the test of time.

Three-Legged Race

My left leg tied to
Your right leg
(run a race like that
and see what you've got)
and I must tell you
how difficult it is
when I see others playing
by different rules!

Putting it Together

Somehow we have built
A family or a semblance of one.
We are the survivors of
Our own private wars.
There is the fear, the grief,
The trauma and the readjustment.
There is human blame here,
And human forgiveness needed.

It is a Struggle

We keep reaching for goals,
Stretching to the limit of
Our endurance, searching,
Finding, in the belief
That somehow something will
Keep us going,
Circumstances will change
Or we will, one or the other.

THE MAZE

Those plants all placed together in the sun
Without the discontent we humans know,
Can be contented with small things they've done,
A stem, a branch, a twig, a bud to grow.
When I restore my life as best I can
And find new ways to grow that give me hope,
I'll maybe come upon a better plan
And then be on the path for which I grope.
One day, I hope that all the pieces fit,
Not just for me, for others too, as well;
Today I'm living just by prayer and wit,
And how it all turns out, just who can tell.
Life has its awkward moments, who can say
How inspiration guides us, when we pray.

TWITCH, TWITCH, TWITCH

Never mind what's wrong with me!
Twitch, twitch, twitch.
We've come here to discuss YOUR problems.
Twitch, twitch, twitch.
If you will just pay attention,
we can get down to business here.
Twitch, twitch, twitch.

The Moccasin, 2000

MOMENTS

Every moment of our lives
The cross-over transits
From the past to the present,
From the present to the future,
From beginnings to substance,
From substance to endings.
As in haiku poetry,
Perhaps the genius of all art,
The real essence of it,
Is the capturing of those
Transitional moments
Within the framework of life.
If every cell of creation
In its brief existence
Is important,
Then every moment we live
Has its part in the continuum,
The moment learning begins,
Or knowing, or understanding
Begins to take hold, not just
In the young child, but
At any time in our lives.

MORNING GLORY

Morning, Gloria!
Your gentle hopes praise God.
Hopes for a better world
Will one day be reality.
Gabriel's floral trumpet blows
Notes unheard by ears.
From your gentle throat
Comes a call
To proclaim the gift of love
That, like the sun and air,
We must all have, to live.
God put his call to glory in
The world,
Little trumpet on the vine.

Moccasin, 2004

THE NEW SNOWFALL

Enter stinging bits of ice, dancing,
Swishing in the cold wind;
Cartwheels of six-sided stars,
An infinity of multiples;
Softer flakes, clinging in clumps,
Big and wet; manna, wedding cake,
Jewels on mittens.

Heavier snow, softening harsh edges
And drifting where the wind blows.
Nature's intermission, freezing
Lakes and ponds.
A time for family life,
Taking inventory, winter sports,
And for some, less traveling
And work.

Ice trekkers, snow blowers,
Long hauls and snowplows,
Inconvenience and a sick child.
But, be too cold, blow too hard,
And fall TOO FAST,
You have an enemy, insidiously subtle,
A BLIZZARD, howling, numbing,
Blinding, hypnotic curtain of death.

NURTURE

A seed becomes a tree,
Becomes a flowering tree,
Becomes a bird nesting
In the tree.

A kindness becomes a
Friendship,
Becomes a bonding,
Becomes a marriage.

A faith becomes blessings,
Becomes fruits of the spirit,
Becomes salvation.

Words and music by Lynn Sorlie, written 2004,
Arranged by Curtis Hanson, John Duss Conservatory, 2005,
Lyrics printed in the Moccasin, 2009

OBSTACLES

I gained when I lost.
More obstacles were put in my path
Because of my intrepid spirit.
The higher the walls, the stronger
My courage, the firmer my will.
Deep convictions rang true.
I didn't give up.

Some who claimed to be religious
Used the Word of God against me,
Twisting its meaning.
Others opposed me and made
No such claim, but I was
A threat to them nonetheless.

It is the same in every age,
The best thinkers too. What a pity.
Then people get the idea that maybe
Someone they persecuted
Had the right idea after all.
The seed goes into the ground
And after a certain time,
Bears fruit.

ON SECOND THOUGHT

Rolling jade green swells
Washing over the wooden ramp...
"Stick yer toe in. It won't hurt yew,"
doesn't persuade me,
sensing shadows in the opaque
green water with its flotsam
and jetsam, floating boards,
seaweed souvenirs.

Nothing small and delightfully
Pretty and tropical, with its markings,
But brown and dirty
From civilization's clutter --
Somewhere an old shoe or a boot.

"No thanks," I say politely,
edging backward,
wishing for a chlorine swimming pool
and its surrounding tiles.

OPPORTUNITY WHEN IT KNOCKS

Stretch out your hand and grab each ray of sun
It will elude you, disappear from view.
Light can't be captured, purchased, stolen, won.
It is ephemeral, playful, warms you.
Ethereal, it travels across space,
Reflected distantly, as on Earth's moon,
Lighting up a seasoned and wrinkled face,
Shining on ocean, mountain, tundra, dune.

It gives each place an opportunity,
Geography and language, skills to teach.
Prospects exist in your community.
Be thankful for the ones within your reach!
Give up the envy, work with what you have
And with your challenges, be brave!

ARROWHEAD POETS, L.O.M.P.
August 2000 2nd Place Award
The Moccasin, 2012, 75th Year

COURAGE

We fear to try, for we may fail,
To love, for we may be rejected,
To die, as we fear punishment or jail,
To live, for what may come upon us.
We fear all things we must overcome,
Inside ourselves, outside ourselves.
This revelation comes to some,
And that is COURAGE.

THE OTHER SIDE OF SUN-NIGHT

A voice or a scent
Is on the mists,
And so faintly
Does its message
Reach my mind
That I'm not sure
If I imagined it.

I send a request
To my mind's deep.
A messenger
Runs out the door
To find you.
There is a way
To reach those we love.

I need no-one else
To make it clear
That my purpose,
As well as yours,
Is to love,
And show it now
In everything we do.

Continued

A whole new life
To share with
The one I love.
Our single purpose
Means so much.
We courageously
Join hands and hearts.

In an ugly world,
Both cynical
And frightening,
We must stand
Firm in our love,
And with you
I fulfill my destiny.

THE ISLAND

Somewhere there is an island in the sea
Where I can think imaginatively,
And I will hear the golden throat of a bird
Singing melodies not yet heard,
And dig for treasure not as yet uncovered –
The truths that are myths until discovered.

Early lyric, written at 15

PEACE IS ELUSIVE

Peace is elusive due to
Man's innate selfishness.
With peace, one can take it
Easy, have more leisure time,
Make money and have more
Possessions, raise a family
That will want even more;
Whereas with war, they will
Have to live with less,
Worry about survival, live
In fear, fight, lose all
The leisure time, possessions,
The good life, to keep
FREEDOM.

The Moccasin, 2009

TRUE GIFTS

The Lord
Has scattered diamonds
From a purse –
Uncut diamonds
Of all sizes
Lying on the road,
Only to melt in the sun.

PEBBLES

For me, life is a problem:

I climb over boulders alright,
No problem there….
It's the pebbles cascading down
And rolling under my shoes
When I climb or descend the
Granite slope, the rocky ledge,
The hill. In front of me lies
Either opportunity, escape,
Or merely convenience.

Any one of them can be so easily
Disrupted by pebbles.

The Moccasin, 2001

PHOTOGRAPHS FOR AN ALBUM

Memories are shared in this album;
Photographs of friends and relatives,
Some who now live *only* in our memories.
We take them out and look at them,
To keep them alive, always.
These bright reminders of continuity
Keep us always bobbing in the raft of hope.
They cushion us from sorrows,
Give us back our youth –
A life raft of family and friends.

PARADOX.

A disparity exists
Between what I think
And what I am;
It also exists
Between what I am
And what I would like to be.
This never changes,
Because I am always changing,
Always growing.

THE PRIMROSE

It was a vision in my mind –
A great, dark church
With stained-glass windows
And east and west wings.
The choirs sang there
In purple velvet robes –
A building like a cross
With old oak pews and beams
And *lantern churches*
Hanging from the ceiling.
Stone tile floors –
Ponderous.

With Grandma MacGregor,
From the balcony I stared
Down into the darkness,
Waiting for "the curtain to go up",
Wondering what I would see,
In this HOUSE OF HOPE.
Then I visualized a garden
Laid out in neat beds
With a central path, a cross,
And here and there, blossoming,
Pale yellow primroses,
The Gardener's.

"She, supposing him to be the gardener,"
said unto him,"
John 20:15

RED

To energize, motivate, propel;
To warn, command, STOP;
To cheer, excite, interest;
To improve, change, re-arrange;
To love, enjoy, cherish;
To make war, destroy, capture;
To covet, desire, want;
To bleed, be injured, die;
To work, play, live --
Red is life, for good or bad;
Red is all these things.

The Moccasin, 2005

VALENTINE

Heart so true, so eloquent –
If you could know how deep I go
To fetch the key that opens up mine –
Oh Love – you would know why
I never thought I had one.

The Moccasin, 2000

REFLECTIONS

In the sunlight on the lake, in a mirror in the light,
We see reflections…
Memories of days gone by, peaceful thoughts of long ago,
Resurrections…
And some things that might have been,
Vain regrets, losses, pain –
Recollections.

In the quiet of the night with the voices down the street,
We hear the laughter…
One loud voice above the rest, guests departing for their cars,
Music follows after…
Couples having a dispute, party chatter, deafening –
Noise to the rafters!

Memories and vain regrets and the loneliness I feel,
Sights and sounds of life…
Words alone cannot express all the feelings in my heart
Thinking of my wife…
Memories surround me here blended in a beautiful
Melody of life.

Written as a poem after my mother died in 1981
A poem about my father's love for my mother
Printed in An Anthology of Poems
By the Arrowhead Poets, 2003
Melody Arranged by Curtis Hanson, 2004

RENEWAL

Oh my life, my life
A tiger has clawed it to ribbons;
No streamers of confetti, but tears,
Paper tears, like old newspaper,
Shredded in boxes marked "fragile".

Survival may depend upon this –
That I overlook a lot.
Maybe then I can recover
What I have nearly lost.
It hurts to look too close.

My mind wanders, seeking
New avenues of hope amidst chaos.
I see this solution here,
I begin to concentrate on life again;
Its force will heal.

Life is purposeful. It will take time.
A new world won't suddenly appear,
But someday, out of this turmoil,
I will stand blinking in the sun,
And the worst will truly be behind me.

RIKKI'S CHINCHILLA FACTORY

One day a relative
Needed a place to stay
I said that she could stay here.
No pets would be allowed,
Of course she understood,
But these were really quite small…

CHORUS

They sleep and rest all day;
At night they eat and play;
They do the Chinchilla Rock.
"Shake, rattle (the cage) and roll!
It's good for your soul!"
They're doing the Chinchilla Rock!

"No, they are not hamsters,
they are raised on ranches.
Five hundred make one fur coat!"
She brought two large cages
With one adjoining ramp.
"They like food pellets and WOOD."

CHORUS

They sleep and rest all day;
At night they eat and play;
They do the Chinchilla Rock.
Shake, rattle (the cage) and roll,
It's good for your soul!"
They're doing the Chinchilla Rock!

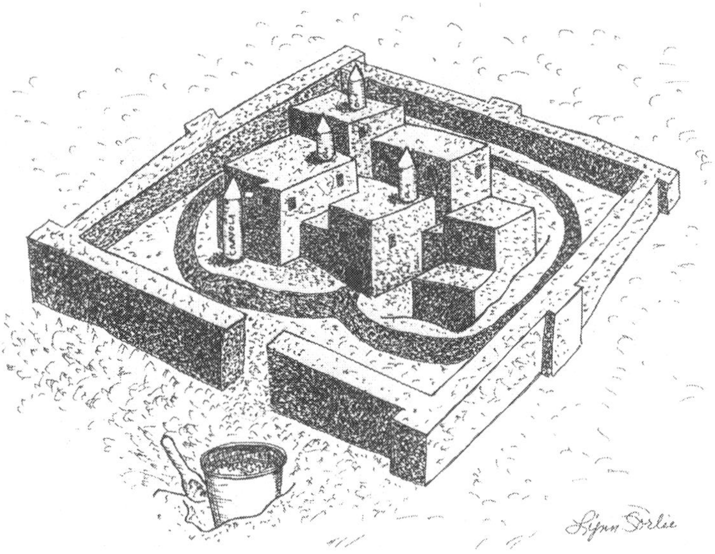

SANDCASTLES in English

What are they building
On that sandpile,
Soon to be destroyed by waves –
Handy like an eraser?

Well, this one shows promise!
Nine or ten years old, these children,
No foolishness.

The old man
Lying now on a beach towel…
Thinking back
To his best sandcastle,
A masterpiece in sculpture
Which was exhibited and won a prize.
It represented to him
All the sandcastles
That would be admired
By a beach gallery.

But these children do not remember
Him, although some here may.
Young hands are building this one.
Maybe there is a future architect
In the group.

Hoosier Challenger, Spring, 1980

CHATEAUX DE SABLE en Francais

Qu'est-ce qu'ils construisent
Sur ce tas de sable,
Bientot detruit par les vagues –
Pratique, comme une gomme?

Eh bien, celui-ci en promet!
Neuf ou dix ans, ces enfants,
Pas de folies.

Le viell homme
Allonge maintenant sur une serviette
De plage repensant
A son meilleur chateau de sable,
Un chef-d'oeuvre en gres,
Qui fut expose et gagna un prix.
Il representait pour lui
Tous les chateaux de sable
Qui seraient admires
Dans une galerie de plage.

Mais ces enfants ne se souvenent
Pas de lui,
Bien que certains ici peuvent.
Des mains jeunes celui-ci construisent.
Peut-etre il y a un futur architecte
Dans le groupe.

SOME GUESTS

Vanity and Pride
Hold court.
Melancholy
Does a solitary
Dance.
Lust and Avarice
Are the life
Of the party.
Resentment
Kicks his partner,
Sudden Anger,
Under the table.
Jealousy does
Not acknowledge
The superb
Performance.

The Moccasin, 2002

SPRING FEVER

I look out the window and see
Carrots.
They seem to be growing in the
Snow
Where I threw them two days ago,
After seeing the white rabbit.

The vegan missiles could have
Scared it,
But the rabbit tracks I saw
Yesterday
Confirmed otherwise.

It has been a very long
Winter.
I look out the window and see
A rabbit,
Like a white ball going by.
They are fast!

But this is April, and time for
SPRING!
Even the rabbit must sense it.

The Moccasin, 2004

THE THRESHOLD

Through the doorway
I can see your form
Waiting for me
Just a little longer –
Not too much longer.

Children who hesitate
To cross the threshold
Will come if bidden,
Needing only reassurance
Of abiding love.

True, I am not a child,
But I cannot forget
My first jump in the pool
With the lifeguard waiting;
I summon my courage.

The Moccasin, 2011

WEATHER SHIFT

The cold is coming down
Like a timber wolf,
With its dark clouds
And wintry wind,
Disturbing the quiet
Beauty of the warm day.

What happened to Spring?
It ran back, like a
Frisky rabbit
Into its burrow,
And like a deer, it
Was quickly gone.

The Moccasin, 2010

SNOW WEAVE

The snow is sketching scenes as it falls,
And cat is looking out the window, watching
Many strange little white hosts become a garment.
Mesmerized by the wind's swift, hurling currents,
He is startled when it swishes past.

The Moccasin, 2010

The Well

There's water in the Rock,
There's water in the Rock,
There's water in the Rock,
It's Jesus!
There's water in the Rock,
There's water in the Rock,
There's water in the Rock,
It's Jesus!

He made this peach to grow
In lands that really show
The meaning of our Christ
In what they do and know.
In them is the Rock.
They're faithful and they know how
To get water from the Rock.

Draw the waters of salvation
Before the final doors are shut
And the water and the thunder
Keeps the other creatures out.

When you know it, you will show it –
That the time is short, my friend,
There is meaning in the outreach,
That we meaningfully extend.

You can't lead a horse to water,
If it doesn't want to drink.
When the summer's hot it will
Feel more inclined, I think.

There's water in the Rock,
There's water in the Rock,
There's water in the Rock,
It's Jesus.
There's water in the Rock,
There's water in the Rock,
There's water in the Rock,
It's Jesus.

Song Lyric, written in 2012

CALLED BACK TO REALITY, Lyric

In my young days, life was fun,
No one took away the sun,
I thought life had just begun.
Trouble turned my life around,
I was not on solid ground,
I was in the Lost and Found.

Sweet diversion, like a snake,
Burning flames out on the lake,
Some folks give, and some folks take.
Called back to reality,
Now of two roads, one I see,
There is just one road for me.

PART II, ESSAY

THE MEANING OF POETRY

THE MEANING OF POETRY

Poetry is an unfolding of the spirit. It is Self-Help therapy. It is a teaching tool, often an essential part of Liberal Arts programs. It is often used for public speaking, in dramatic presentations and toastmaster ceremonies. It is used for public causes and issues. History was passed down in memorized poetic forms. In this way, stories and legends were spread before the printing press was invented.

Many cultures contributed to the wealth of poetry made available today, written in the style or form of their time. The Shakespearean Sonnet was written during the dramatic and literary period of William Shakespeare, in England, though Shakespeare was best known for his plays. He wrote tragedies and comedies for king and queen and the common people. His influence helped to unify and forge a great nation.

Japanese Haiku is another form. Usually 17 syllables, and three lines, each word important, it expresses the sentiments of the season. Season words are used, invoking strong images, such as our 4th of July. Traditional Japanese art compliments its haiku in style.

Art History helps us to understand basic trends that resulted in styles of the times. Regarding the realism and dramatic power of the movies, music and art of this generation, maybe poetry needs to embrace this trend to be effective.

Are we moving too fast to have time to think eloquently? No, I don't think so. On the contrary, some of the best poetry has come from the cities. Read Carl Sandburg's poems about his beloved Chicago. A poet can be found anywhere.

Poetry wears many masks. There are comedies and tragedies, classic and modern. There are cute, silly verses and profound utterances. There may be many voices in a chorus or only one. The styles vary considerably, from English romantic poetry to plain, homely American poets like Robert Frost. The complex language of Emily Dickinson is hard to duplicate.

There is poetry without words. A photograph or drawing may capture it. The theme may be painful and tragic or beautiful and fulfilling. There is poetry in dance alone, and in mime – silent gestures and movements in a dramatic presentation. Marcel Marceau was one of the best.

There is poetry in the flight of birds and a different kind of poetry in the movements of the great fish of the sea. It isn't any *one* thing, but it's one thing separated out.

Poetry is beautiful, and the only reason I can think of as to *why* it isn't appreciated more in this culture, is that it's seen as a weakness instead of a strength!

More To Be Said About Poetry

Poetry is a flower, a mood, a prayer, or a tender moment. It is a benediction, a gift, a hymn, a presentation, a performance.

Poetry has courage and organization. It marshals words as a noble challenge or a humble pledge.

As humor, it rises a little above things, as praise or ornament, it makes us thankful.

It gives us something to wear, so we may go before the King.

III, HAIKU

Spring, Summer, Fall, Winter

"The poems that appeal most to me here are those in which you display a sense of humor and are striving more to make a point than for poetic effect."

"Some of the shortest poems seem to me the best. I think because you have a single focus, whether it be a simple insight or an evocative image."

Dave Driscoll, college writing instructor

Bee & Flower

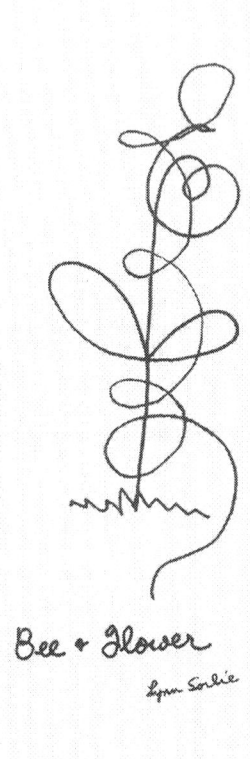

Lynn Sorlie

SPRING

Jaunty tulip *cups*
On sturdy, straight, sheathed stems
That children can draw.

Coming home to see
Snowshoe bunnies chasing round
--making a circle.

The Moccasin, 2012

The abundant rains
Have brought out many creatures
Like that little fox.

The Moccasin, 2008

The Mississippi
Leaving devastation behind
Returns to its banks.

The Moccasin, 2011

The new baseball team
Proud in their new uniforms;
"Now, let's see them play!"

The Moccasin, 2009

A gaunt coyote
Tracking a wild animal
Disappears up the trail.

In the melting snow
The deer again find pathways
To my shrubbery.

February thaw…
Remembering that snow is
Water after all.

The Moccasin, 2003

A flat-bottom boat
On the frozen, reedy lake
-- to rescue a fawn.

Late February;
Cloud bands puff out like cotton
Near the sunrise.

Underlit by dawn
Rosy clouds near Pilot Knob
Suggest needed rain.

Pastels intermixed
With layered cloud formations;
Waiting for rain.

A Great Blue Heron
Flies over canoe classes
Near Yuma.

Planting lettuce rows;
Unionized men and women
-- dressing better.

Tree with fluffy balls
Fragrant in the Yuma breeze
-- in this arid land.

Tiny alyssum
A sturdy edging plant;
-- my hands are clumsy.

Plucky petunias
Delicate in appearance
Will take summer's heat.

Abundant blossoms
On Cranberry Viburnums
Promise the birds food.

The Moccasin, 2011

A walk in the woods;
Seeing this small star-flower
With seven petals.

In the old peach tree
An empty oriole's nest
Swings with the breeze.

Woodland dogwood trees
Gracefully turn their petals
In southern curtseys.

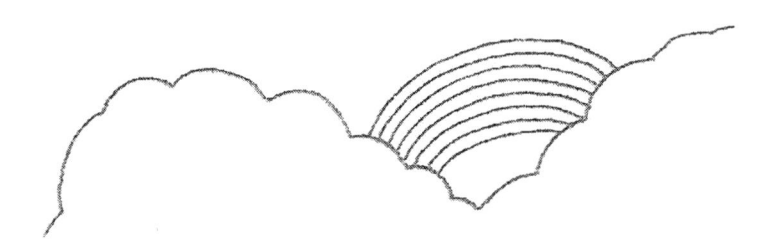

SUMMER

Heavy gusting winds;
A young swimmer gets thrown
By a plastic horse.

Along the highway
The tall, tufted field grass
Dips and sways.

A dip in the lake;
Coming up with eyes open
Toward the surface.

Small paddle-wheel boats
Going out on Lake Como
From the pavilion.

Inside the movies;
The MGM lion's roar
Competes with thunder.

Dragonfly Haiku, October 1982

Billowing clouds
As far as the eye can see;
Endless becoming…

Cumulus clouds
Covering vast distances
Build changing shapes.

Oshkosh far below;
White glints on a wash of blue
Mark a regatta.

San Pedro cliffs;
Hang gliders in slow motion
Ride the thermals.

From the small airplane
Summer stars and lights below
Seem as one.

A hummingbird
Attracted to a flower
Called, "Butter and Eggs."

On a Wild One's tour;
A Lady's-slipper Orchid
In the cedar swamp.

A Black Bear outside
Only this one is mature
-- just looking around…

At Wisconsin Dells;
Riding the duck boat trail
The group spots a fawn.

Cedar swamp tour;
A Dragon's-mouth Orchid
Near the bog trail.

Sunflower tops
Mournfully absent one day
Because of the deer.

A seaplane landing
Silently across the lake;
Faint eastern light.

Cloudless dawn;
Drone of a fisherman's boat
Crossing the lake.

A day so still…
Reluctant to dip an oar
Into the water.

Not a wisp of breeze
On this sultry afternoon;
The splash of a fish.

Hoosier Challenger, Spring-Summer 1979

August stillness;
Even nature has to stop
And listen to it.

The Moccasin, 2000

No one wants to talk
When the summer stillness
Seems to say it all.

Perfectly still,
Silence makes its own sound
On this August day.

Add nothing to
This perfect summer day
Nor take it away.

"The sound of silence"
is very loud today
-- putting words to shame.

The Moccasin, 2000

Bluejays quickly claim
The Arrowwood Viburnum's
Blue berries

At the pop concert;
There is nothing quite as nice
Out under the stars.

At a safe distance
We watch the barge of fireworks
This Fourth of July.

The Moccasin, 2010

Summer night cloudburst;
Running feet on the pavement
Outside the movies.

Dragonfly Haiku, April 1975
Minnesota Moccasin, 2010

At Powderhorn Park;
Crysanthemum candlebursts
-- blue, white, red...

Hoosier Challenger, Winter 1980-81
The Moccasin, 2011

Harbor lights shimmer;
Boarding outgoing vessel
People pack fun in.

"Caps" on the sidewalk
-- we hit them hard with a rock;
I remember…

Worth every penny
-- the joy on a child's face
when fireworks explode!

At the baseball field;
After an evening game
Fireworks begin!

Steep cliffs either side;
"MILE HIGH LEMON MERINGUE PIE"
Catches our eye.

Colorado storm;
A cow pony herding sheep
High in the sky.

Dragonfly Haiku, October 1982 AWARD

Sierra foothills;
Headlights trace the route ahead
To California.

Fountain in the Mall;
Delighted, the old vagrant
Dunks his head in.

Foothills barbecue;
Where private lots with trailers
Become a way of life.

Beavers slap their tails
Letting us know we're too close
To their river homes.

A night bird swoops low
Causing me to mistake it
At first, for a bat.

Fat upside-down bug
And the smell of a skunk
Near the water dish.

San Pedro harbor;
Prowling on adobe walls,
Herman makes the rounds.

Unstable coastline
-- that "ziggedy" one-eighth mile,
pipes above the ground…

Fine ash on the car…
Carried aloft by the winds
From distant fires.

FALL

School starting soon;
Children play in inner tubes
Beyond the dock.

September morning;
A bittern stands stock-still
By the roadside.

September sunset;
A glass and steel skyscraper
In reflected light.

Rat-tat-tat-tat-tat;
A Red-headed Woodpecker
Drills the telephone pole.

A wild grape vine
Dresses up an old elm tree
This crisp September.

Squirrels zig-zag
-- cut across stately shadows
on the leaf-strewn lawn.

The aspen forest;
Startled grouse are flushed out
When we walk through it.

The days are colder;
Coming in from the garden
With a last bouquet.

Too windy to be out;
Suddenly, a grouse crash-lands
In our window well.

Very few hunters
Are allowed to shoot pheasant
In these corn fields.

October school day;
Breezes stir up maple leaves
And turn book pages.

Glowing deer eyes
Line the clearing near the road
-- hearing the whistle.

A shot is heard, then,
"NO HUNTING, GET OFF MY LAND!"
rings through the woods.

"Giant harvesters
collect grain from those fields
to feed the world."

A walk through the park;
A thick layer of oak leaves
Under the bare trees.

Startled by a moose
Loping past our window, then…
Down the forest path.

Early November;
Each spruce seems to have its own
Resident squirrel.

The newspaper stand;
A sudden blast of cold wind
-- one more day ripped off.

Cemetery pond;
The Mallard ducks and wild geese
Have departed.

The mournful eyes
Of the old sea turtle
Longing for the sea.

Harvest fruit
Pickled and spiced for winter;
Thanksgiving bounty.

WINTER

High in the Sierras;
A lighted cabin obscured
By swirling snow.

Snow piled on snow
In the high mountain passes;
Avalanche warning.

Two old pines
Lean against each other
Under heavy snow.

The Moccasin, 2011

The wonder dog
Leaping high into the air
To catch snowballs.

Poor part of town;
Girl in a second-hand mink
And blue jeans.

Hoosier Challenger, Summer-Fall 1978

Sparkle-lit snow
With diamond-like brilliance
Almost blinds the eyes.

A cardinal flits
From tree to tree to tree
After heavy snow.

A friend with a sled
And the cover goes back on
The jig-saw puzzle.

The bill collector
Wants all of his money;
Christmastime.

Raiding the bird feeder
A marten climbs up the tree
-- a strange silhouette.

Undulating drifts
Of snow smooth out the hills;
She puts the brush down.

Sheets of ice
Make walking treacherous;
"Winter Wonderland."

Gingerly, the cat
On crusted snow, makes his way
Toward the bird sound.

The Moccasin, 2012, 75th Year

Winter Carnival;
King Boreus' Ice Palace
Dressed in colored lights.

The Moccasin, 2012, 75th Year

The air is so cold;
It shatters with the shrill bark
Of a little dog.

The Moccasin, 2012, 75th Year

Will Steger boots
The "last word" in winter wear
Here in the Northland!

Deer in a long line
Cross a small frozen lake
Late in the winter.

The Moccasin, 2010

Late winter at dusk;
A Great Grey Owl swoops down
And seizes a mouse.

The Moccasin, 2010

THE END

Made in the USA
Columbia, SC
31 July 2018